SPIRITUAL HUNGER

FILLING YOUR DEEPEST LONGINGS

8 Studies for Individuals or Groups

JIM AND CAROL PLUEDDEMANN

SHAW

WATERBROOK
PRESS

SPIRITUAL HUNGER
A SHAW BOOK
PUBLISHED BY WATERBROOK PRESS
12265 Oracle Boulevard, Suite 200
Colorado Springs, CO 80921

Unless otherwise indicated, all Scripture quotations are taken from
the *Holy Bible: New International Version* ® *NIV* ® Copyright 1973,
1978, 1984 by International Bible Society. Used by permission of
Zondervan Publishing House. All rights reserved.

ISBN: 978-0-87788-770-6

Published in the United States by WaterBrook Multnomah, an imprint
of The Doubleday Publishing Group, a division of Random House
Inc., New York

SHAW and its circle of books colophon are registered trademarks
of Random House Inc.

Cover photo © 1993 by Robert Moseley

Printed in the United States of America

146502721

CONTENTS

INTRODUCTION

What is the greatest desire of your life, the deepest longing of your being? You may not recognize your longing as spiritual hunger, but a yearning for God was built into you at creation. Augustine expressed this when he said, "Thou hast made us for Thyself, and our hearts are restless until they rest in Thee." If you try to satisfy your thirst for God with a substitute, you will thirst all the more.

God created us to be spiritual as well as physical beings. So it's no wonder that we have spiritual longings. But what is true spiritual hunger? If you log onto the Internet and type "spiritual" on a search engine, you'll find thousands of book titles and products. Yet much that is labeled "spiritual" is human-centered rather than God-centered. Still, the emptiness and restlessness each human soul experiences can be like a signpost that points to the feast only God can give.

God himself has given us that spiritual desire, and he longs to fill it. Richard Foster observes: "God, you see, rushes to us at the first hint of our openness. He is the hound of heaven baying relentlessly upon our track. He places within us such an insatiable God hunger that absolutely nothing satisfies us except the genuine whole-wheat Bread of Life." Or as A. W. Tozer puts it, "We pursue God because and only because He has first put an urge within us that spurs us to the pursuit."

The psalmist invites us to "taste and see that the Lord is good" (Psalm 34:8). Amazingly, the more we feast on God the more we hunger for him. The paradox is beautifully expressed by Bernard of Clairvaux:

We taste Thee, O Thou living Bread,
And long to feast upon Thee still:
We drink of thee, the Fountainhead
And thirst our souls from Thee to fill.

But what if you don't feel a hunger for God? If righteousness isn't the passion of your life at this point, don't despair. You were created to know and love God. Your deepest longings can only be filled by him, and he is continually reaching out to you. Ask God to give you a healthy spiritual appetite. Ask him to help you want righteousness as much as a starving person wants food and a person dying of thirst wants water.

HOW TO USE THIS STUDYGUIDE

Fisherman studyguides are based on the inductive approach to Bible study. Inductive study is discovery study; we discover what the Bible says as we ask questions about its content and search for answers. This is quite different from the process in which a teacher *tells* a group *about* the Bible, what it means, and what to do about it. In inductive study, God speaks directly to each of us through his Word.

A group functions best when a leader keeps the discussion on target, but this leader is neither the teacher nor the "answer person." A leader's responsibility is to *ask*—not *tell*. The answers come from the text itself as group members examine, discuss, and think together about the passage.

There are four kinds of questions in each study. The first is an *approach question*. Used before the Bible passage is read, this question breaks the ice and helps you focus on the topic of the Bible study. It begins to reveal where thoughts and feelings need to be transformed by Scripture.

Some of the earlier questions in each study are *observation questions* designed to help you find out basic facts—who, what, where, when, and how.

When you know what the Bible says, you need to ask, *What does it mean?* These *interpretation questions* help you to discover the writer's basic message.

Application questions ask, *What does it mean to me?* They challenge you to live out the Scripture's life-transforming message.

Fisherman studyguides provide spaces between questions for jotting down responses and related questions you would like to raise in the group. Each group member should have a copy of the studyguide and may take a turn in leading the group.

For consistency, Fisherman guides are written from the *New International Version.* But a group should feel free to use the NIV or any other accurate, modern translation of the Bible such as the *New Living Translation,* the *New Revised Standard Version,* the *New Jerusalem Bible,* or the *Good News Bible.* (Paraphrases of the Bible may be referred to when additional help is needed.) Bible commentaries should not be brought to a Bible study because they tend to dampen discussion and keep people from thinking for themselves.

SUGGESTIONS FOR GROUP LEADERS

1. Read and study the Bible passage thoroughly beforehand, grasping its themes and applying its teachings for yourself. Pray that the Holy Spirit will "guide you into truth" so that your leadership will guide others.

2. If the studyguide's questions ever seem ambiguous or unnatural to you, rephrase them, feeling free to add others that seem necessary to bring out the meaning of a verse.

3. Begin (and end) the study promptly. Start by asking someone to pray for God's help. Remember, the Holy Spirit is the teacher, not you!

4. Ask for volunteers to read the passages out loud.

5. As you ask the studyguide's questions in sequence, encour-

age everyone to participate in the discussion. If some are silent, ask, "What do you think, Heather?" or "Dan, what can you add to that answer?" or suggest, "Let's have an answer from someone who hasn't spoken up yet."

6. If a question comes up that you can't answer, don't be afraid to admit that you're baffled! Assign the topic as a research project for someone to report on next week.

7. Keep the discussion moving and focused. Though tangents will inevitably be introduced, you can bring the discussion back to the topic at hand. Learn to pace the discussion so that you finish a study each session you meet.

8. Don't be afraid of silences; some questions take time to answer and some people need time to gather courage to speak. If silence persists, rephrase your question, but resist the temptation to answer it yourself.

9. If someone comes up with an answer that is clearly illogical or unbiblical, ask him or her for further clarification: "What verse suggests that to you?"

10. Discourage Bible-hopping and overuse of cross-references. Learn all you can from *this* passage, along with a few important references suggested in the studyguide.

11. Some questions are marked with a ♦. This indicates that further information is available in the Leader's Notes at the back of the guide.

12. For further information on getting a new Bible study group started and keeping it functioning effectively, read Gladys Hunt's *You Can Start a Bible Study Group* and *Pilgrims in Progress: Growing through Groups* by Jim and Carol Plueddemann.

SUGGESTIONS FOR GROUP MEMBERS

1. Learn and apply the following ground rules for effective Bible study. (If new members join the group later, review these guidelines with the whole group.)

2. Remember that your goal is to learn all that you can *from the Bible passage being studied.* Let it speak for itself without using Bible commentaries or other Bible passages. There is more than enough in each assigned passage to keep your group productively occupied for one session. Sticking to the passage saves the group from insecurity and confusion.

3. Avoid the temptation to bring up those fascinating tangents that don't really grow out of the passage you are discussing. If the topic is of common interest, you can bring it up later in informal conversation following the study. Meanwhile, help each other stick to the subject!

4. Encourage each other to participate. People remember best what they discover and verbalize for themselves. Some people are naturally shier than others, or they may be afraid of making a mistake. If your discussion is free and friendly and you show real interest in what other group members think and feel, they will be more likely to speak up. Remember, the more people involved in a discussion, the richer it will be.

5. Guard yourself from answering too many questions or talking too much. Give others a chance to express themselves. If you are one who participates easily, discipline yourself by counting to ten before you open your mouth!

6. Make personal, honest applications and commit yourself to letting God's Word change you.

A THIRST FOR GOD

Psalm 63

When we lived in Nigeria, we often went hiking with our family and friends. One day we set out to find a waterfall that one of our pilot friends had seen from the air. "An easy morning's hike," he said. We took off with water canteens and plans to hike three or four hours. But we lost our way and ended up walking all day under a hot sun, never finding the promised waterfall. Our water supply was quickly used up, and the few small streams we saw were not safe to drink from. Aching with weariness, we learned that day what it means to thirst in "a dry and weary land where there is no water."

David wrote Psalm 63 in the Desert of Judah when he was fleeing from his son Absalom. His desert experience became a picture of his soul's longing and thirst for God. Perhaps it will describe your yearning as well.

1. How would you describe your spiritual thirst at this point in your life?

Read Psalm 63.

2. What words and images does David use to describe the intensity of his desire for God (verse 1)?

◆ 3. How might David's words reflect his circumstances and surroundings at this time in his life?

◆ 4. In a sense, verse 1 describes a paradox: David *has* God, yet he also *seeks* him. How do you find this paradox at work in your relationship with God?

5. Why is David determined to praise God, even in parched and cheerless surroundings (verses 2-4)?

6. Note the strong contrast between verses 1 and 5. When have you known intense thirst or rich satisfaction in your spiritual journey?

7. When you wake up in the night and can't sleep, what do you tend to think about?

How can David's example encourage you (verse 6)?

◆ **8.** How does verse 8 describe the human/divine interplay of our relationship with God? (What is our role? What is God's role?)

9. In verses 9-10 David's thoughts return to his present situation. What does he recognize about the ultimate destiny of his enemies?

◆ **10.** Though temporarily banished as king, what hope does David express in verse 11?

11. Which verse of this psalm best expresses your relationship with God?

What encouragement does this psalm give you for deepening your desire for God?

Going Deeper

One of the early church fathers, St. John Chrysostom, advised reading this psalm every day. For the next week, make a commitment to read Psalm 63 daily. Next time you meet as a group, reflect together about how the daily reading of this psalm affected you.

SOUL FOOD

Isaiah 55

At the end of World War II, Coca-Cola's president proclaimed his company's ultimate goal—*that everyone in the world have a taste of Coke.* Christians might benefit from comparing Coca-Cola's "Great Commission" with our own. Are we committed to giving everyone in the world an opportunity to taste the water and bread of life? This is the invitation of Isaiah 55. It reminds us that only as we nurture our souls with spiritual food will we be truly filled.

1. Do you normally think of God as someone who wants to give you

—bread and water?

—a bland but nourishing meal?

—a sumptuous banquet?

Explain your answer.

Read Isaiah 55:1-7.

2. List all the words in these verses that express actions God wants his people to take.

What overall impression do these words make on you?

3. Do you ever feel you are spending your "money on what is not bread, and your labor on what does not satisfy" (verse 2)? Explain.

◆ 4. The word "come" is used five times in the first three verses. What does this indicate about the nature of human beings and their role in the salvation process?

♦ **5.** What promises does God make to those who respond to him (verses 1-7)?

♦ **6.** This passage is addressed to the Jews, God's people in exile. What do verses 4 and 5 suggest about God's purposes for the rest of the world?

♦ **7.** What is implied by the phrases "while he may be found" and "while he is near" (verse 6)?

8. What requirement is involved in turning to God (verse 7)?

Read Isaiah 55:8-13.

9. How do verses 8 and 9 make you feel about God?

10. To what is the word of the Lord compared (verses 10-11)? Why is this an apt image?

In what ways have you seen this principle at work in your life or in someone else's life?

11. What will God's people experience as they are restored (verse 12)? To what end?

12. What artistic form would you choose to express the meaning of the promises in verses 12-13 (art, music, dance, writing, photography)? Why?

13. In what ways have you been trying to satisfy your spiritual appetite with junk food?

What steps can you take to come to the Lord and feed regularly on his Word?

Going Deeper

Reflect this week on the spiritual nourishment you are receiving. Is it adequate? Satisfying? If not, begin to obey the commands of Isaiah 55—come, eat, listen, hear, seek, turn to the Lord. Ask God to guide your plans for spiritual nurture and to help you in carrying out those plans.

QUENCHING YOUR THIRST

John 4:1-42

Malcolm Muggeridge, a British journalist, experienced much fame, success, and pleasure in his life. What did he think about it?

> I may, I suppose, pass for being a relatively successful man. People occasionally stare at me in the streets—that's fame. . . . It might happen once in a while that something I said or wrote was sufficiently heeded for me to persuade myself that it represented a serious impact on our time—that's fulfillment. Yet I say to you—and I beg you to believe me—multiply these tiny triumphs by a million, add them all together, and they are nothing . . . measured against one draught of that living water Christ offers to the spiritually thirsty, irrespective of who or what they are.

In John 4, Jesus offers that living water to a spiritually thirsty woman. His invitation is also open to us and to our seeking friends.

1. What are some of the "tiny triumphs" you have experienced in life?

How satisfying have these been to you?

Read John 4:1-26.

◆ 2. Asking for water on a hot day seems like a very normal request. What made Jesus' request surprising (verses 4-9)?

What barriers exist between people today that are similar to those which Jesus crossed to talk to this woman?

3. Look at each reference to water in verses 10-15. How does Jesus use the woman's physical interest in water to teach spiritual truth?

4. In what ways might physical or emotional desires reveal deeper spiritual needs within ourselves or our friends?

◆ **5.** Why do you think Jesus brings up the woman's personal life (verses 16-18)?

◆ **6.** The woman quickly changes the subject, hoping that Jesus will resolve a theological debate between the Samaritans and the Jews (verses 19-20). How does Jesus' answer go beyond what either side had envisioned as true worship?

7. How does worshiping God quench our deepest longings?

8. John 4:26 is the first time on record that Jesus reveals himself as Messiah. How does it strike you to know Jesus chose this woman as the first person to hear this announcement?

Read John 4:27-42.

9. What effect do Jesus' words have on the woman (verse 28-29)? On the whole town?

10. What similarity do you see between the disciples' misunderstanding about food (verses 31-34) and the woman's misunderstanding about water?

11. How can doing God's will provide the same essentials in our spiritual lives as food does for our physical bodies (verse 34)?

◆ **12.** What can we learn about effective witnessing from Jesus' conversation with this woman?

13. If Jesus were to stop by and share a cup of coffee with you, what might he ask you about your life right now?

What would you ask him?

Going Deeper

How can you "drink" this week of the living water Jesus offers? Spend time in personal worship. Then think about people you know who are searching for answers in their lives. How might you start where they are and help them move to new levels of spiritual interest as Jesus did with the Samaritan woman?

SATISFYING YOUR HUNGER

John 6:25-40

Often it seems that our lives are focused on food—earning money to be breadwinners, grocery shopping, cooking, eating, cleaning up. And no matter how satisfying a meal may be, we're always hungry again. Peter Kreeft writes, "Everyone, not just 'religious people' (whoever they are), is born, built, and designed to feed on God-food; and when we try to feed on other food, we starve."

Jesus tried to help his listeners think about something more important than free food. He claimed he could satisfy the deepest hunger of the soul—forever.

1. How would you describe your typical spiritual diet— Slim-Fast®? Meat and potatoes? Junk food? Fresh-baked bread? Leftovers? Baby food? Frozen convenience food? Explain your answer.

Read John 6:25-40.

2. What motivates the crowd to search for Jesus (verse 26; see also John 6:10-14)?

What self-centered motives might cause people to follow Jesus today?

◆ 3. Look at each of the questions asked by the crowd (verses 25, 28, 30, 34) and at each of Jesus' responses.

Question	Response

4. How did the people's concerns differ from Jesus' concerns?

Why do you think their interests were so far apart?

5. The Jews were always interested in doing good works (verse 28). How does the "work" God requires differ from what they might have expected (verse 29)?

◆ **6.** The Jews believed that when the Messiah came, he would give manna as Moses did in the Old Testament. How does Jesus use the crowd's physical hunger to whet their spiritual appetites (verses 32-33)?

7. What does Jesus mean when he says that he is the bread of life (verses 35-40; see also verses 48-51)?

8. List all the other claims and promises Jesus makes here (verses 35-40). Which of these do you find most meaningful right now? Why?

◆ **9.** Jesus' teaching about the bread of life is closely linked to his death on the cross. What facts about eternal life can you learn from this passage?

10. Notice again the divine/human interplay in verse 44. How were you drawn to Jesus?

What was your original motive in coming to Jesus? Did you resist coming to him?

11. We often think of eternal life only as something to be received at the moment of salvation. Yet in what sense must we continually come to Christ to satisfy our spiritual hunger and thirst?

12. What might you do this week to increase your spiritual appetite?

How can others support you in prayer?

Going Deeper

This week, pay special attention to your spiritual diet and keep a record of your spiritual food. Are you feeding on any other "junk food" that might be curbing your spiritual appetite? Are you taking in enough spiritual food to keep you healthy and growing? Ask God to give you a greater hunger for him and his Word and to show you ways to enrich your spiritual diet.

STREAMS OF LIVING WATER

John 7:37-44; Acts 1:4-11; 2:1-13

If you are feeling empty and inadequate, you may be on the verge of a great adventure with Jesus. Recognizing our need and spiritual longing can be a blessing as we realize the distance between who we are and who we can become. When we come to a place where we are empty and broken, we are ready to be filled. And when we are filled, our lives can then flow out to others with blessing.

1. Describe a time when you very much wanted to communicate an important message but felt hampered or inadequate to do so.

Read John 7:37-44.

Note: The setting for this passage is the Feast of Tabernacles, one of the most important and joyful feasts celebrated by the Jews. Each day of the feast a priest in Jerusalem took a golden pitcher to the Pool of Siloam, filled it with water, then carried it back through the Water Gate while the people recited Isaiah 12:3: "With joy you will draw water from the wells of salvation." Perhaps it was at this dramatic moment when Jesus called out to the crowd, "Come to me and drink."

♦ **2.** How does the symbolic use of water at the feast add significance to Jesus' words in verses 37-38?

3. How does John explain the meaning of "living water" and its effect on those who drink it (verses 38)?

♦ **4.** Why would this new work of the Spirit begin only after Jesus had been glorified (that is, after his death, resurrection, and ascension)?

5. What different reactions do the people have to Jesus' words?

How do these reactions compare to typical contemporary responses to Jesus?

Read Acts 1:4-11.

6. What is the promised gift Jesus speaks of in verses 4 and 5? (Review Jesus' description of this gift in John 7:38-39.)

7. Compare and contrast being baptized with water and being baptized with the Spirit. How are they similar? different?

♦ **8.** Christians often desire the gift of the Holy Spirit in order to fulfill their spiritual longings. What did Jesus say would be the bigger purpose of this gift (verse 8)?

9. What do you learn about the scope of God's kingdom from verse 8?

How does this contrast with the disciples' view in verse 6?

Read Acts 2:1-13.

10. In what different ways was the gift of the Holy Spirit demonstrated (verses 2-4)?

♦ **11.** Describe the miracle of communication that took place among the international throng of people.

How did this fulfill the purpose of the gift described in Acts 1:8?

12. Cite the various reactions of the crowds to this event. (Note the parallel to John 7:40-44.)

13. Water that doesn't flow becomes stagnant. In what ways has Christ's living water satisfied your spiritual thirst and then flowed out to others?

Going Deeper

God wants to fill you with his Holy Spirit so that you can be a witness to those who are still hungry and thirsty. Look again at Acts 1:8. Where is your Jerusalem? Your Judea and Samaria? Your ends of the earth? How will you have an active part in being a witness to each of these spheres?

FEEDING THE HUNGRY

Isaiah 58:1-12

Lloyd Ogilvie, Chaplain to the U.S. Senate, tells of a woman who was experiencing a time of spiritual dryness and was anxiously seeking the power of the Holy Spirit for her life. Ogilvie asked her to identify ten people who needed her love and ministry in their lives. When she became involved in specific, sacrificial ways of caring for these people, the Holy Spirit empowered her. As she reached out, her reward was an intensive, intimate experience of the Spirit of God.

Isaiah 58 explores this spiritual principal of giving and receiving. It may hold some surprises for you as you look for ways to satisfy spiritual hunger.

1. What do you think about fasting? If you have fasted before, what benefits or pitfalls did you experience?

Read Isaiah 58:1-7.

♦ 2. What "right things" do God's people seem to be doing (verses 1-3)?

3. What is wrong with their religious activity (verses 3-5)?

4. Describe the kind of fasting God wants (verses 6-7).

5. The Beatitudes in Matthew 5 speak of "hungering and thirsting after righteousness." How does this relate to the kind of fasting God wants (verses 6-7)?

Read Isaiah 58:8-12.

6. About whom or what is God most concerned in this passage?

7. List the "if-then" statements God makes.

According to this passage, how is spiritual well-being connected with reaching out to meet the needs of others (verses 8-12)?

8. What images does Isaiah use to describe the results of extending mercy and compassion to others?

Why are these fitting images for these truths?

◆ **9.** Which do you think comes first: spiritual renewal or outreach? Why?

◆ **10.** In what areas of spiritual activity do you feel that you are just going through the motions (Bible reading, church attendance, fasting, praying, tithing, etc.)? According to this passage, what might need to change?

◆ **11.** What kinds of hunger do human beings have?

What would it mean for you to "spend yourselves in behalf of the hungry" (verse 10)?

12. Someone has said that evangelism is "one beggar telling another where to get bread." Do you agree? If so, how might you reach out to people you know in this way?

13. How has this passage shed light on your understanding of satisfying spiritual hunger?

Going Deeper

Isaiah speaks of God's people as "Repairers of Broken Walls" (verse 12). What might this mean for us today? Keep in mind that we live in a broken world and that God has called us to a ministry of reconciliation (2 Corinthians 5:19-20). How will you be a "Repairer of Broken Walls" this week?

LONGING FOR HOME

Philippians 3

"If I find in myself a desire which no experience in this world can satisfy, the most probable explanation is that I was made for another world." C. S. Lewis penned those words to help explain what he called the "inconsolable longing" human beings feel for heaven.

The apostle Paul expressed the same yearning in Philippians 3. "Our citizenship is in heaven," he said. "And we eagerly await a Savior from there." Knowing Christ was the passion of Paul's life. Is it ours?

◆ 1. Are there times when you find yourself feeling homesick for heaven? What prompts those feelings most?

Read Philippians 3:1-11.

◆ **2.** What reasons does Paul have for putting "confidence in the flesh" (verses 3-6)?

3. How might social status, personal accomplishments, religious heritage, or even pious acts lead us to rely on ourselves rather than on Christ?

4. Missionary martyr Jim Elliot said, "He is no fool who gives what he cannot keep to gain what he cannot lose." What does Paul lose (verses 7-8)?

What does he gain (verses 7-11)?

◆ **5.** Paul knew *about* Christ even before he was converted. What do you think he means in verse 10 when he says, "I want to know Christ"?

6. How might sharing in Christ's sufferings contribute to Paul's goal of knowing Christ?

Read Philippians 3:12-16.

◆ **7.** Paul compares himself to a long-distance runner. How does he view his progress in the race?

◆ **8.** What is Paul's goal, and how does he plan to reach it?

◆ **9.** What were some of the things Paul needed to forget in his past (verse 13)?

10. Practically speaking, how can we benefit from the past, yet also "forget what is behind"?

11. Paul had a single-minded focus: "One thing I do: . . ." How can you be more focused in your commitment to Christ so that this same kind of vision characterizes your life?

Read Philippians 3:17-21.

12. What contrast does Paul make between people whose minds are on earthly things and people whose minds are on heaven?

13. What difference might it make to you this week to live as a citizen of heaven instead of living as though this world is all there is?

Going Deeper

In Philippians 3 Paul reviews his past (verses 1-11), his present (verses 12-16), and his future (verses 20-21). Summarize briefly what he says about each of these phases in his life. Then make a time line of your life, graphing the highs and lows in your spiritual journey so far. As you reflect on your past, present, and future, keep your spiritual citizenship in view. Do your priorities and ambitions reflect your true citizenship?

FILLED TO OVERFLOWING

Revelation 21:1-8; 22:1-17

The last two chapters of the Bible give a spectacular, totally satisfying conclusion to the quest of every human heart. In heaven, all of our longings will be fulfilled forever.

As you study the following passages, ask God to give you "eyes of faith" to anticipate the glorious reality of heaven, where your thirst will be quenched completely.

1. What do you most look forward to about heaven?

Read Revelation 21:1-8 and 22:1-6.

2. The writer (John) speaks about a new heaven and a new earth. What are these new features as described in these passages?

3. What will *not* be found in heaven?

4. As you read this description of heaven, what appeals most to you? Why?

◆ **5.** What is the requirement for drinking the water of life (verses 21:6 and 22:17)?

Why do you think this is all that's required?

◆ **6.** Scan Genesis 2:4-17 and compare it to the passages in Revelation you just read. What similarities do you notice in the two accounts? What differences?

How do you feel about the new heaven being a city rather than a quiet garden?

Read Revelation 22:7-17.

◆ **7.** Who will live in the new Jerusalem (verses 21:7 and 22:14)?

Who will not live there (verses 21:8 and 22:15)?

◆ **8.** Do you think it's ever too late for a person to receive God's offer of salvation (verse 11)? Why or why not?

◆ **9.** What can you learn about Jesus from the names he gives himself in verses 13 and 16?

10. God's great invitation to "Come!" is repeated twice in verse 17. What keeps people from accepting this invitation?

11. As you end these studies, take time to thank God for his gracious invitation and for his free gift of living water.

Going Deeper

Who, in your circle of friendships, still needs to hear Jesus' invitation? As you thank God for his gift of living water that fills our spiritual longings, pray for those you know who are thirsting. Ask God to give you opportunities to share his gracious invitation with them. As you plan your activities for the weeks ahead, make sure this priority is reflected in your schedule.

LEADER'S NOTES

■ **Study 1/ A Thirst for God**

Question 3. Most scholars think this psalm was written when David was fleeing from Absalom rather than from Saul because verse 11 refers to David as "king." Second Samuel 15:13-14, 23-26 tells the painful story of David's estrangement from his son Absalom and his escape to the desert. David left behind his family, his throne, and the ark of God's covenant—the symbol of God's presence. Now he found himself in the desert where the parched earth became a picture of his own experience.

Question 4. Martyn Lloyd-Jones helps us to understand this paradox: "The Christian is one who at one and the same time is hungering and thirsting, and yet he is filled. . . . That is the blessedness of this Christian life. . . . It goes on and on; perfect, yet not perfect; hungering, thirsting, yet filled and satisfied, but longing for more, never having enough because it is so glorious and so wondrous" *(Studies in the Sermon on the Mount,* p. 83. London: InterVarsity Press, 1974).

Question 8. David clings steadfastly to God, yet it is God himself who makes this possible by holding David in his strong right hand. This is a beautiful and vivid description of the human/divine roles in mutual relationship.

Question 10. David knows that his calling as king is from God. Use of the royal title "becomes a reassertion of his calling, which was from God, and an avowal that this cannot fail" (Derek Kidner, *Psalms 1–72,* Tyndale Old Testament Commentary Series, p. 227. Leicester, U.K.: InterVarsity Press, 1977).

■ Study 2/Soul Food

Question 4. "God provides salvation freely for everyone who thirsts, but He calls upon sinners to come. . . . Man is not a mere automaton. Life is real. Decisions are real. Man has to make choices and is responsible for the choices he makes. God made man a rational and moral creature, and expects him to use his mind and govern his will" (Allan A. MacRae, *The Gospel of Isaiah,* p. 162. Chicago: Moody Press, 1977).

Question 5. Encourage group members to look carefully at God's promises in these verses. His gift is available to all; it is offered freely, is permanent, satisfying, and life-giving. Remember that this was written for God's people in exile, a time when the people had to pay even for water (see Lamentations 5:4).

Question 6. The attraction of nations to the God of Israel is a major biblical theme. Israel was to be a "light to the nations," and all the nations are blessed because of Israel's Messiah.

Question 7. "Now is the day of salvation. These verses imply that a time will come when it will no longer be available. For some the return of Christ will mean the beginning of a new and joyous existence. For others it will mean the end of all opportunity to accept God's gracious invitation" (Allan A. MacRae, *The Gospel of Isaiah,* p.166).

■ **Study 3/Quenching Your Thirst**

Question 2. In Jesus' day, Jews and Samaritans were taught to despise each other from birth, but Jesus broke this barrier and approached a Samaritan. He also crossed a gender barrier by talking to a woman. Rabbis were not allowed to greet a woman in public, even if the woman was the rabbi's wife or daughter. In addition, this woman had a questionable reputation. This may be the reason she came to the well alone at the hottest time of day.

Question 5. When Jesus tells the woman about her personal history, she begins to grasp that he has supernatural power. The reminder of her tragic life also increases her thirst for living water.

Question 6. In some ways, the woman was well-informed about Jewish beliefs, and it is significant that Jesus respected her and carried on a theological discussion with her. The rabbis despised women and thought them incapable of receiving any real teaching. Jesus helped her understand that the place of worship was not the important issue. The greatest importance is to worship in spirit and in truth. "True and genuine worship is not to come to a certain place; it is not to go through a certain ritual or liturgy; it is not even to bring certain gifts. True worship is when the spirit, the immortal and invisible part of man, speaks to and meets with God, who is immortal and invisible" (William Barclay, *The Gospel of John,* Vol. 1, p. 154. Edinburgh: St. Andrew Press, 1969).

Question 12. Two testimonies led the people of Sychar to believe—the woman's testimony and their own personal encounter with Jesus Christ. Today it is the same. People need to hear about Christ from those who know him and be led to a personal discovery of their own. As effective witnesses, we should begin as Jesus did with commonplace needs and turn these into conversations with eternal implications.

■ **Study 4/Satisfying Your Hunger**

Question 3. The people were only interested in physical satisfaction. Jesus wanted to draw them to a spiritual level and to a
recognition of their true hunger. It was difficult for the people
to understand the symbolism of the bread of life. But there may
have been a sense in which they did not *want* to believe. "Many
people reject Christ because they say they cannot believe he is
the Son of God. In reality, the claims he makes on their lives
are what they can't accept. So to protect themselves from the
message, they deny the Messenger" *(Life Application Bible,* p.
251. Wheaton, IL: Tyndale House Publishers, 1987).

Question 6. Jesus reminds the crowd that it wasn't Moses who
gave them manna; it was God. Then he shows that the manna
was physical and temporal. It could not satisfy their need for
eternal life like Jesus, the bread of life could do.

Since the people were interested in food, Jesus used that
interest to lead them to a spiritual interest in eternal food. Just
as bread is essential for physical life, Jesus is essential for eternal life. Food isn't a luxury. Just as our physical life depends on
food, our spiritual life depends on Jesus.

Question 9. This passage is rich with salvation themes. God is
the one who provides salvation through his Son (John 6:33).
But just as bread must be eaten, we must come to Jesus and
believe on him in order to receive salvation (verse 35).
Whoever comes will not be driven away (verse 37). Salvation
provides eternal life and resurrection from the dead (verse 40).
No one can come to Jesus unless the Father draws him (verse
44). Jesus gave his body on the cross for the life of the world
(verse 51).

■ **Study 5/Streams of Living Water**

Question 2. "It was as if Jesus said: 'You are thanking and glorifying God for the water which quenches the thirst of your bodies. Come to Me if you want water which will quench the thirst of your soul.' Jesus was using that dramatic moment to turn men's thoughts to the thirst for God and for eternal things" (William Barclay, *The Gospel of John,* Vol. 1, p. 262).

Question 4. John explained that the "living water" was the coming gift of the Spirit. Though the Holy Spirit was active prior to this time, he had not yet been given to indwell believers permanently. This happened after Jesus' death, resurrection, and ascension at the Day of Pentecost.

Question 8. "The power of the Holy Spirit will be given for a very specific purpose: to be a witness. The energizing, life-giving Spirit is for communication. . . . There are lots of people today who are seeking the gifts and power of the Holy Spirit for their own needs. That's only the beginning" (Lloyd J. Ogilvie, *Acts of the Holy Spirit,* pp. 22–23. Wheaton, IL: Shaw Publishers, 1999).

Question 11. The "tongues" described here are probably different from the ecstatic utterances Paul discusses in 1 Corinthians 12–14. "The words spoken at Pentecost under the Spirit's direction were immediately recognized by those who heard them as being languages then current, while at Corinth no one could understand what was said till someone present received the gift of interpretation" (Richard N. Longenecker, *The Expositor's Bible Commentary, Acts,* p. 67. Grand Rapids, MI: Zondervan, 1995).

■ Study 6/Feeding the Hungry

Question 2. It may seem that God is addressing his people harshly, but they have rebelled continually since being freed from slavery in Egypt. The book of Isaiah begins with a description of Israel's rebellion. God says, "I reared children and brought them up, but they have rebelled against me. . . . Ah, sinful nation, a people loaded with guilt, a brood of evildoers, children given to corruption! They have forsaken the Lord; they have spurned the Holy One of Israel and turned their backs on him" (Isaiah 1:2, 4). Because of their long history of rebellion, God allowed his people to be taken captives in Babylon. Isaiah's message is one of judgment as well as hope. God will bring Israel back to be his worshiping people again.

Question 9. One of the best ways to grow in our walk with God is to minister to others. Outreach and growth go hand in hand. It's not necessary to "have it all together" spiritually before we reach out to others. As we reach out, we experience more light (verse 10), our own needs are satisfied (verse 11), and our thirst is quenched (verse 11).

Question 10. "When you strive to be a spiritual person, you fight the constant battle of 'ritual versus reality.' It is much easier to go through the external activities of religion than it is to love God from your heart and let that love touch the lives of others" (Warren Wiersbe, *The Essential Everyday Bible Commentary,* p. 964. Nashville: Thomas Nelson, 1993).

Question 11. People experience hunger at many levels, but their ultimate need is for spiritual food from God himself. The most loving thing we can do for others is bring them to Jesus, the bread of life.

■ Study 7/Longing for Home

Question 1. C. S. Lewis observed that our deepest longings for heaven aren't necessarily prompted by suffering or unhappiness. Instead, it's often when we experience the best of earthly pleasures—a sunset, a symphony, or intimate love—that we long for something more. Lewis says, "It was when I was happiest that I longed most."

Questions 2 and 3. "Righteousness was the great goal of Paul's life when he was a Pharisee, but it was a self-righteousness, a works righteousness, that he never really could attain. . . . When Paul trusted Christ, he saw God put Christ's righteousness to his own account! . . . Many religious people will not even admit they *need* any righteousness. Like Saul of Tarsus, they are measuring themselves by themselves, or by the standards of the Ten Commandments, and they fail to see the *inwardness of sin*" (Warren W. Wiersbe, *Be Joyful: A Practical Study of Philippians,* p. 89. Wheaton, IL: Victor Books, 1982).

Question 5. When Paul was a Pharisee persecuting the church, he knew about Christ. But now he longs for a personal relationship based on faith, not merely on knowledge.

Question 7. Paul has a "sanctified dissatisfaction" about his spiritual condition. He knows he is not perfect and that he has to keep pressing on. "Many Christians are self-satisfied because they compare their 'running' with that of other Christians, usually those who are not making much progress. . . . But Paul did not compare himself with others; he compared himself with *himself* and with *Jesus Christ*" (Warren Wiersbe, *Be Joyful,* p. 95).

Question 8. Note that Paul is not talking about attaining salvation here. That would contradict what he said earlier about not trusting his own works or self-effort for salvation. As citizens of heaven, we are responsible to run the race God has given us. Once again we see the divine/human interplay here. "I take hold of that for which Christ Jesus took hold of me."

Question 9. Paul had reason to feel guilty—he actively persecuted the Christians before his conversion. But he didn't brood over his past. Warren Wiersbe points out that in Bible terminology, "'to forget' does not mean 'to fail to remember.' Apart from senility, hypnosis, or a brain malfunction, no mature person can forget what has happened in the past. . . . So, 'forgetting those things which are behind' does not suggest an impossible feat of mental and psychological gymnastics by which we try to erase the sins and mistakes of the past. *It simply means that we break the power of the past by living for the future.* We cannot change the past, but we can change the meaning of the past" (Warren Wiersbe, *Be Joyful*, p. 98).

■ Study 8/Filled to Overflowing

Question 5. There is no cost for the water of life. The requirement is to be thirsty!

Question 6. Notice the river and the tree of life in each account. In the Genesis account the river flows through a garden, and in the Revelation account it flows through a city. In the first creation Adam was forbidden to eat from the tree of life. In the new creation the tree yields fruit every month for the satisfaction of God's people, without any curse.

Question 7. "It is Jesus Christ who in His Cross has provided that grace and that sacrifice by which man alone can be forgiven; but man has to appropriate that sacrifice; he has to wash his own robes, as John would put it, in the blood of Jesus Christ. To take a simple analogy, we can supply soap and water, but we cannot compel a person to use them. So those who enter into the city of God are those who have accepted and appropriated the sacrifice of Jesus Christ" (William Barclay, *The Revelation of John,* Vol. 2, p. 290. Edinburgh: St. Andrew Press, 1966).

Question 8. "There comes a time when a man is so set in his character that all that any situation can do is to make him more deeply and more ineradicably what he is. Therein lies the human tragedy—that a man can so long refuse the way of Christ that in the end he cannot take it. That, in fact, is the sin against the Holy Spirit" (William Barclay, *The Revelation of John,* p. 287).

Question 9. "He is, in two words, both the *root* and *offspring* of David, both his ancestor and his descendant. . . . He encompasses the whole of history. Then, as the *bright morning star* he heralds the dawn of eternity, telling us that this life is only the prelude to the real life of the world to come" (Michael Wilcock, *I Saw Heaven Opened: The Message of Revelation,* p. 218. Downers Grove, IL: InterVarsity Press, 1975).

WHAT SHOULD WE STUDY NEXT?

To help your group answer that question, we've listed the Fisherman Guides by category so you can choose your next study.

TOPICAL STUDIES

Angels, Wright

Becoming Women of Purpose, Barton

Building Your House on the Lord, Brestin

The Creative Heart of God, Goring

Discipleship, Reapsome

Doing Justice, Showing Mercy, Wright

Encouraging Others, Johnson

The End Times, Rusten

Examining the Claims of Jesus, Brestin

Friendship, Brestin

The Fruit of the Spirit, Briscoe

Great Doctrines of the Bible, Board

Great Passages of the Bible, Plueddemann

Great Prayers of the Bible, Plueddemann

Growing Through Life's Challenges, Reapsome

Guidance & God's Will, Stark

Heart Renewal, Goring

Higher Ground, Brestin

Images of Redemption, Van Reken

Integrity, Engstrom & Larson

Lifestyle Priorities, White

Marriage, Stevens

Miracles, Castleman

One Body, One Spirit, Larsen

The Parables of Jesus, Hunt

Parenting with Purpose and Grace, Fryling

Prayer, Jones

The Prophets, Wright

Proverbs & Parables, Brestin

Satisfying Work, Stevens & Schoberg

Senior Saints, Reapsome

Sermon on the Mount, Hunt

Spiritual Gifts, Dockrey

Spiritual Hunger, Plueddemann

A Spiritual Legacy, Christensen

Spiritual Warfare, Moreau

The Ten Commandments, Briscoe

Ultimate Hope for Changing Times, Larsen

Who Is God? Seemuth

Who Is the Holy Spirit? Knuckles & Van Reken

Who Is Jesus? Van Reken

Wisdom for Today's Woman: Insights from Esther, Smith

Witnesses to All the World, Plueddemann

Women at Midlife, Miley

Worship, Sibley

What Should We Study Next? continued

BIBLE BOOK STUDIES

Genesis, Fromer & Keyes
Exodus, Larsen
Job, Klug
Psalms, Klug
Proverbs: Wisdom That Works, Wright
Ecclesiastes, Board
Jeremiah, Reapsome
Jonah, Habakkuk, & Malachi, Fromer & Keyes
Matthew, Sibley
Mark, Christensen
Luke, Keyes
John: Living Word, Kuniholm
Acts 1–12, Christensen
Paul (Acts 13–28), Christiansen
Romans: The Christian Story, Reapsome
1 Corinthians, Hummel

Strengthened to Serve (2 Corinthians), Plueddemann
Galatians, Titus & Philemon, Kuniholm
Ephesians, Baylis
Philippians, Klug
Colossians, Shaw
Letters to the Thessalonians, Fromer & Keyes
Letters to Timothy, Fromer & Keyes
Hebrews, Hunt
James, Christensen
1 & 2 Peter, Jude, Brestin
How Should a Christian Live? (1, 2 & 3 John), Brestin
Revelation, Hunt

BIBLE CHARACTER STUDIES

Abraham, Reapsome
David: Man after God's Own Heart, Castleman
Elijah, Castleman
Great People of the Bible, Plueddemann
King David: Trusting God for a Lifetime, Castleman
Men Like Us, Heidebrecht & Scheuermann

Moses, Asimakoupoulos
Paul (Acts 13–28), Christensen
Women Like Us, Barton
Women Who Achieved for God, Christensen
Women Who Believed God, Christensen

Printed in the United States
by Baker & Taylor Publisher Services